MUSIC READINESS SERIES

MY COLOR AND PLAY B

by
Betty Glasscock and Jay Stewart
in collaboration with David Carr Glover
editorial assistance by Carole Flatau
illustrations by Bob Blansky

Dedicated to Ethel Pfeiffer and her daughters, Jeanne and Kathleen.

FOREWORD

MY COLOR AND PLAY BOOK A is for the very young child who has completed MY FIRST MUSIC BOOK of the MUSIC READINESS SERIES. The book is designed to guide the student in the development of musical awareness, motor skills and recognition of music symbols. MY PIANO BOOK A will guide the student in developing keyboard skills.

A Program Guide of Concepts and Activities for MY COLOR AND PLAY BOOK A and MY PIANO BOOK A is on pages 42-45 of MY COLOR AND PLAY BOOK A.

MY COLOR AND PLAY BOOK A is correlated with MY PIANO BOOK A. The abbreviation (MPB-#) is placed at the bottom right hand corner of each page to indicate the corresponding pages to be used from MY PIANO BOOK A.

Upon completion of MY COLOR AND PLAY BOOK A and MY PIANO BOOK A, it is recommended that the student continue musical study with the MY COLOR AND PLAY BOOK B and MY PIANO BOOK B.

TO THE PARENT: Your role is very important. You will need to encourage the student to spend time each day practicing the keyboard skills and responding to rhythm patterns by clapping, playing a rhythm instrument or playing at the keyboard. The teacher will suggest other activities that will reinforce the concepts and skills presented at the lesson.

You can help make this a successful and happy experience. Encourage and praise your child frequently. Provide opportunities for listening experiences — records, radio, concerts, singing. When possible, the parent should attend the lesson with the student.

TO THE TEACHER AND PARENT: The CASSETTE TAPE RECORDING of the MUSIC READINESS SERIES includes all the keyboard and singing songs. The songs are presented in sequential order as their titles or page references appear in the Program Guide, pages 42-45.

This recording will be helpful to the teacher in class as melodic lines, rhythm ensembles, or suggested body movements are demonstrated and explored with the songs.

Listening to the recording at home will aid the parent and student as words, rhythms, and melodies of the songs are reinforced.

CONTENTS

Special thanks to teachers and students of the Glover Music Village for their willingness and enthusiasm in testing this series.

2

My Music Review

1. Draw a circle around each two-black key group on the keyboard at the top of this page.
2. Hold up your hands and wiggle the correct finger as your teacher calls out finger numbers.
3. Draw a line from each picture at the bottom of the page to the correct clef sign for high or low sounds.

See FOREWORD for explanation of this cue.
(MPB 4,5)

4

MY MUSIC REVIEW

1. Clap the rhythm pattern and say the counts aloud.

1. Draw a circle around each of the three-black key groups at the top of this page.
2. Clap the rhythm pattern and say the counts aloud.
3. Circle each group of quarter notes that go up.
4. Circle each group of quarter notes that go down.

(MPB 4,5)

MY MUSIC REVIEW

1.

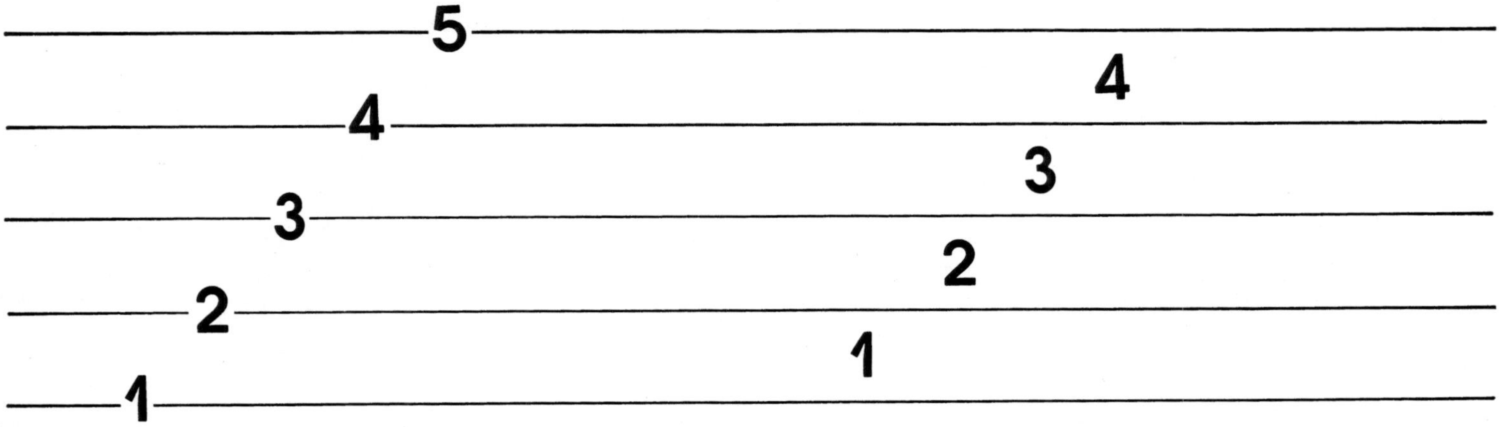

2.

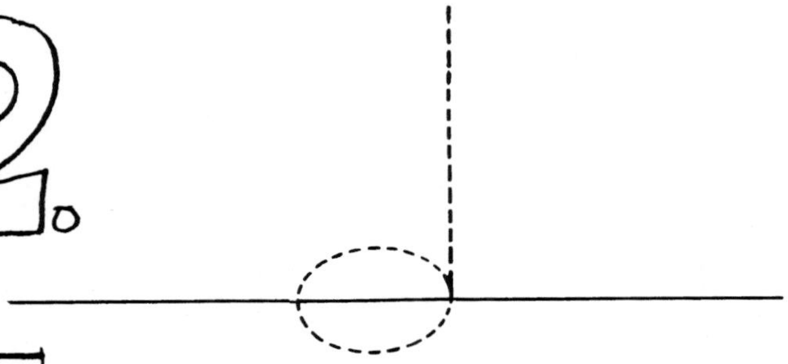

3.

4.

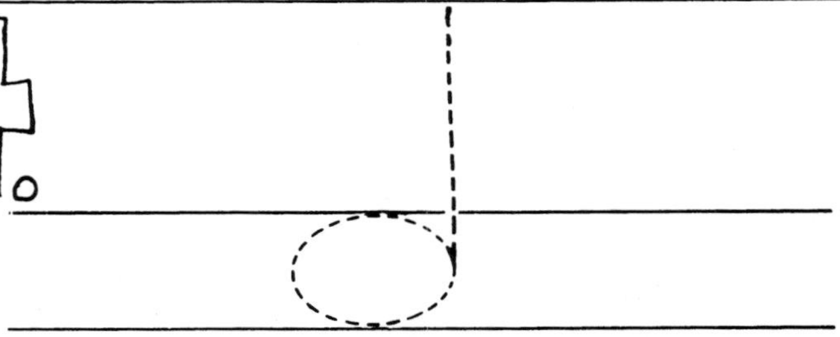

5.

1. Review staff lines and spaces by pointing to the correct line or space as your teacher says, "line 2, space 4" etc.
2. Draw on the dotted lines to make a line note.
3. Draw two line notes on the staff.
4. Draw on the dotted lines to make a space note.
5. Draw two space notes on the staff.

(MPB 4, 5)

CHARLIE'S MIDDLE C

1. Draw on the dotted lines to make Charlie's Middle C note.
2. Draw a line from Charlie's Middle C note to the Middle C key on the keyboard.
3. Draw on the dotted lines to make the letter C.
4. Circle finger 1 on the right hand pictured above.
5. Locate Charlie's Middle C on the keyboard and play it with right hand finger 1.

(MPB 6.7)

CHARLIE'S RHYTHM PATTERNS

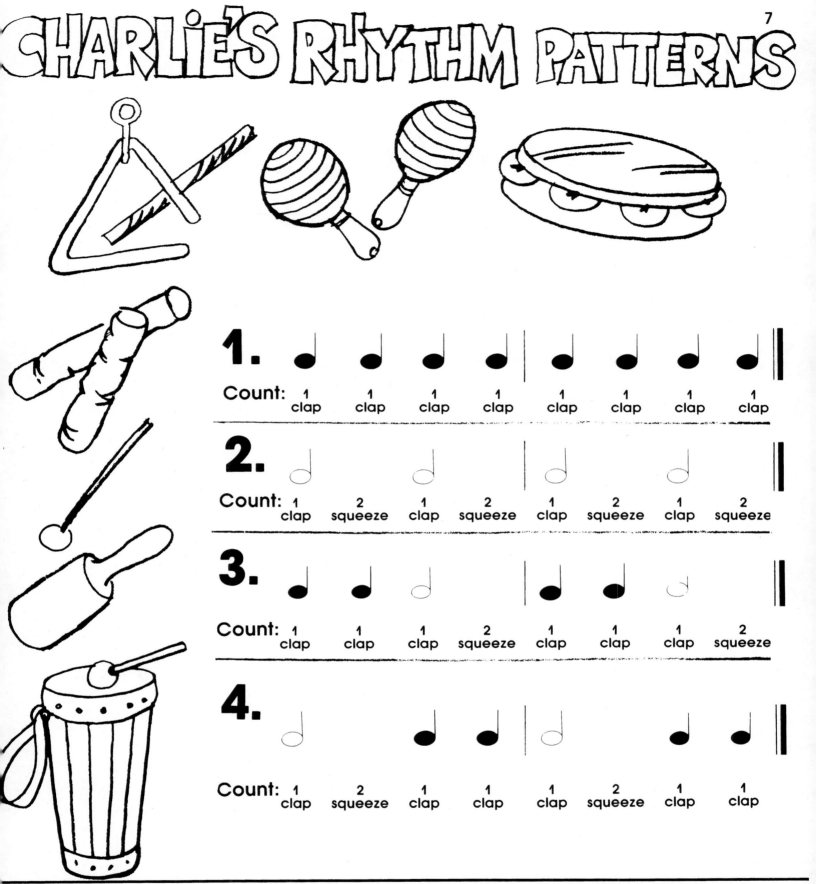

1.

Count:
1 clap | 1 clap | 1 clap | 1 clap | 1 clap | 1 clap | 1 clap | 1 clap

2.

Count:
1 clap | 2 squeeze | 1 clap | 2 squeeze | 1 clap | 2 squeeze | 1 clap | 2 squeeze

3.

Count:
1 clap | 1 clap | 1 clap | 2 squeeze | 1 clap | 1 clap | 1 clap | 2 squeeze

4.

Count:
1 clap | 2 squeeze | 1 clap | 1 clap | 1 clap | 2 squeeze | 1 clap | 1 clap

1. Clap the rhythm patterns and say the beats aloud. Clap and say "one" on the quarter note. Clap and say "one" on the half note; squeeze your hands together as you say "two".
2. CHALLENGE! Choose line 2, 3 or 4 to be your "solo" line. As the group continues to clap line 1, students take turns playing their "solo" lines.
3. EXTRA CHALLENGE! Clap line 1 and continue to repeat it. When your teacher points to line 2, 3 or 4 all the students who chose that as their "solo" line clap that line once and then go back to line 1.
4. EXTRA EXTRA CHALLENGE! Have an ensemble. Some students clap their "solo" line while others play their "solo"- line on rhythm instruments or on Charlie's Middle C.

DANKA'S D

MIDDLE C

D

1. Draw on the dotted lines to make Danka's D note.
2. Draw a line from Danka's D note to the D key on the keyboard.
3. Draw on the dotted lines to make the letter D.
4. Circle finger 2 on the right hand pictured above.
5. Locate Danka's D on the keyboard and play it with right hand finger 2.

(MPB 8,9)

CHARLIE'S C and DANKA'S D

1. Mark an X on each C on the keyboard at the top of the page.
2. Mark an X on each D on the keyboard at the bottom of the page.
3. EXTRA FUN: Play "Find That Key." Students stand with their backs to the keyboard. When teacher calls out "C" or "D", students turn to the keyboard and play the correct key. Example: "the highest C on the keyboard, the next D below Middle C, etc."

3144   (MPB 10)

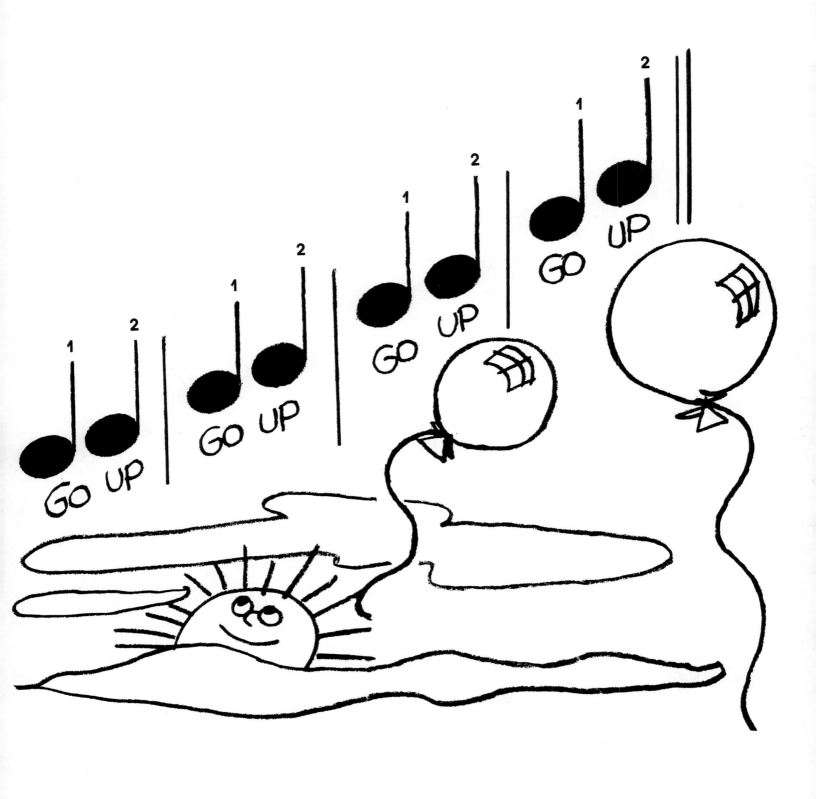

1. **Find the lowest C and D on the keyboard. If you have a floor keyboard, stand on the lowest C and D and hop to the next C and D.**
2. **Using right hand fingers 1 and 2, play all the Cs and Ds going up the keyboard. Stand and walk as you play. Say "C,D" as you play the keys. Play again, saying "Go up" as you play.**
   (Teacher: Introduce technic for two-note phrasing. Have students <u>drop</u> on finger 1 and <u>lift the wrist</u> with an upward motion on finger 2.)

Ellen's E

1. Draw on the dotted lines to make Ellen's E note.
2. Draw a line from Ellen's E note to the E key on the keyboard.
3. Draw on the dotted lines to make the letter E.
4. Circle finger 3 on the right hand pictured above.
5. Locate Ellen's E on the keyboard and play it with right hand finger 3.

Color the picture. As you color, make up a short story about the things in the picture. Perhaps the children were frightened by the noises the animals made outside their tent. Decide which sounds would be good to help tell the story. Use keyboard sounds, rhythm instruments, voices, paper rattling-anything that makes sounds you like. Practice telling the story with the sounds. (The teacher may be the storyteller while the students make their sounds.)

Record the story so you can listen to it. You might like to perform the story for another class or for your family or friends.

(MPB 13)

C D E

STEPPING UP

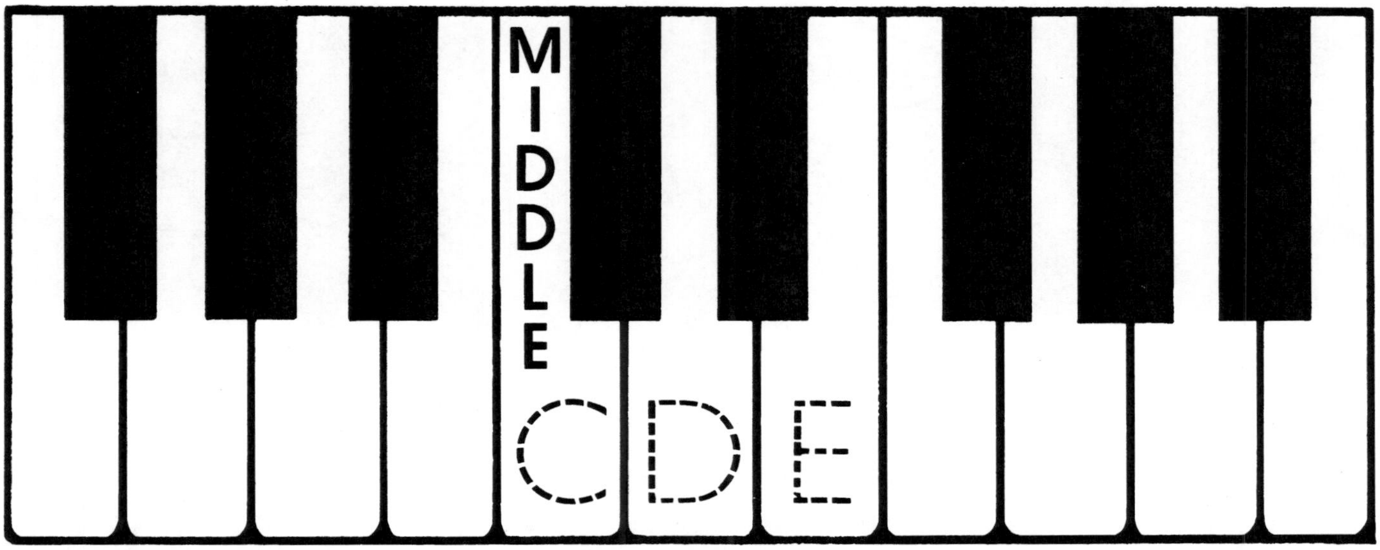

MIDDLE

C D E

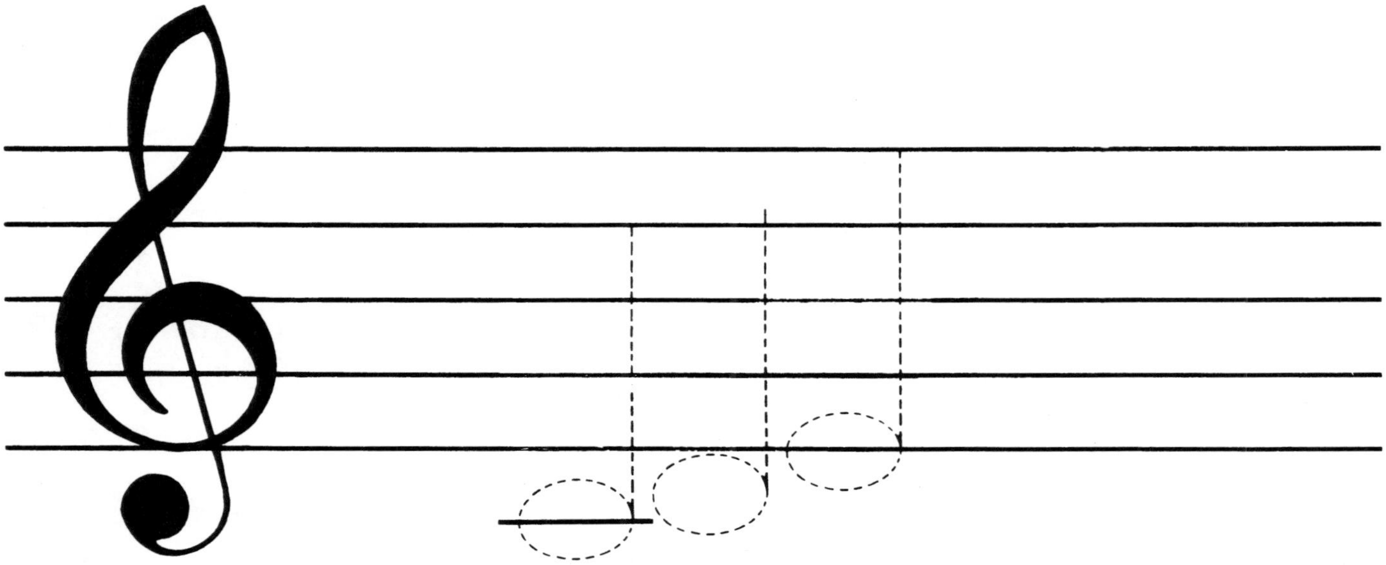

Count: 1 1 1 2

Clap: Clap Clap Clap Squeeze

Sing: C D E _____

Sing: Step—ping up _____

1. Draw on the dotted lines to make the notes C, D, and E.
2. Color C and D black, making them quarter notes.
3. Draw a line from each note to the correct key on the keyboard above.
4. Count and clap the rhythm.
5. Play and count aloud.
6. Play and sing the letter name of each note.
7. Play and sing the words.

(MPB 14)

E D C STEPPING DOWN

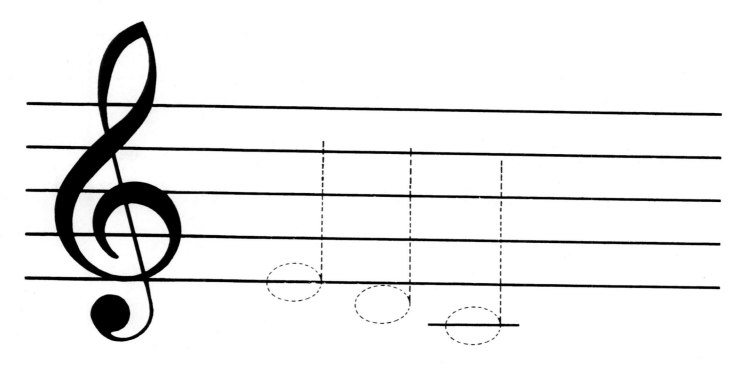

Count:	1	1	1	2
Clap:	Clap	Clap	Clap	Squeeze
Sing:	E	D	C	_____
Sing:	Step — ping		down	_____

1. Draw on the dotted lines to make the notes E, D, and C.
2. Color notes E and D black, making them quarter notes.
3. Count and clap the rhythm.
4. Play and count aloud.
5. Play and sing the letter names.
6. Play and sing the words.

NOTES C, D and E

C D E D E

1. Draw on the dotted lines to make letter names for the notes C, D, and E.
2. Play the correct key on the keyboard as your teacher points to a note. Say the note name as you play the note.
3. NOTE GAME: The teacher assigns a note to each student. As the teacher points to a note, all students assigned that note stand up. A student who stands for the wrong note is out of the game.

(MPB 15)

FiFi's F

1. Draw on the dotted lines to make Fifi's F note.
2. Draw a line from Fifi's F note to the F key on the keyboard.
3. Draw on the dotted lines to make the letter F.
4. Circle finger 4 on the right hand pictured above.
5. Locate Fifi's F on the keyboard and play it with right hand finger 4.

EL 3144

(MPB 16, 17, 18, 19)

GOMEZ' G

1. Draw on the dotted lines to make Gomez' G note.
2. Draw a line from Gomez' G note to the G key on the keyboard.
3. Draw on the dotted lines to make the letter G.
4. Circle finger 5 on the right hand pictured above.
5. Locate Gomez' G on the keyboard and play it with right hand finger 5.

(MPB 20, 21)

C D E F G STEPPING UP

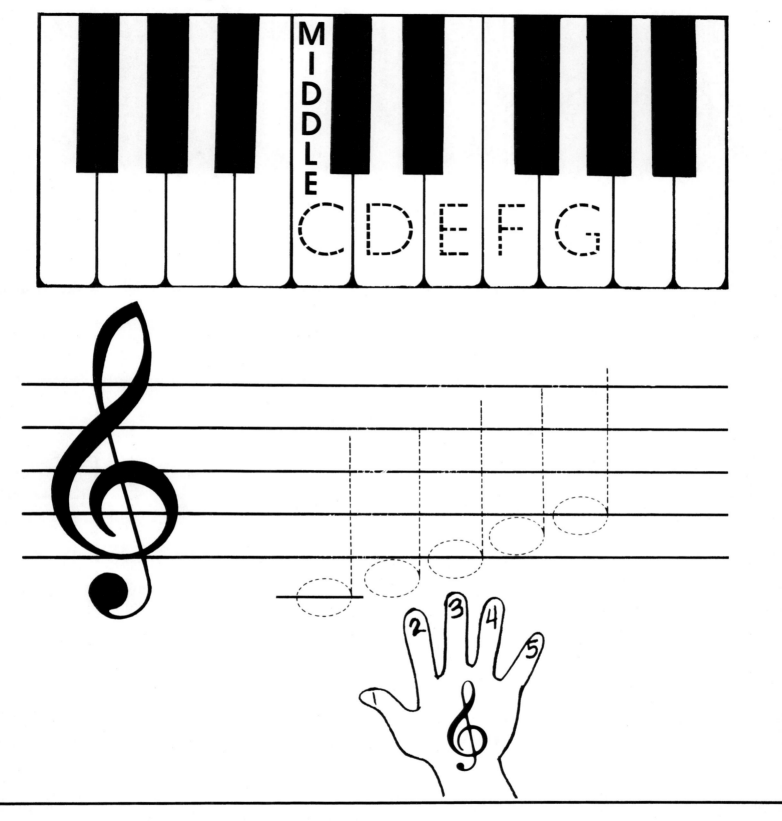

1. Draw on the dotted lines to make the notes C, D, E, F, and G.
2. Make them quarter notes.
3. Draw a line from the note C to the key C on the keyboard at the top of the page. Draw a line from the note D to the D key. Continue for E, F, and G.
4. Draw a line from the C note to finger 1 of the right hand.
   Draw a line from the D note to finger 2 of the right hand.
   Continue for E, F, and G.
5. Place your hand over the keys C, D, E, F, and G. Play the correct key as your teacher points to a note.

WHOLE NOTES

Count: 1 2 3 4 | 1 2 3 4 | 1 2 3 4 | 1 2 3 4

Clap: Clap   Squeeze | Clap   Squeeze | Clap   Squeeze | Clap   Squeeze
          Squeeze   Squeeze | Squeeze   Squeeze | Squeeze   Squeeze | Squeeze   Squeeze

1. Draw on the dotted lines to make whole notes. Practice drawing whole notes at the chalkboard.
2. On the floor keyboard stand on a key and pretend to be a whole note as the class counts "1, 2, 3, 4." On the first count of each new note move to a new key.
3. Clap and count whole notes. On the first beat clap and say "one". Squeeze your hands together for beats "two, three, four."
4. Play whole notes at the keyboard. Remember to hold the key down for all four counts.

(MPB 23)

EASY C D E F G SONG

1. **Place your right hand fingers on the keys C, D, E, F, G.**
2. **Play and sing EASY C D E F G SONG.**

Char - lie play on C   Dan - ka play on D   El - len play on E

Fi - fi play on F   Go - mez play on G   G F E D C

CHARLIE'S RHYTHM REVIEW

1. count: 1   1   1   2 | 1   2   3   4
clap: clap   clap   clap   squeeze   clap   squeeze   squeeze   squeeze

2. count: 1   1   1   2 | 1   1   1   2
clap: clap   clap   clap   squeeze   clap   clap   clap   squeeze

3. count:
clap   clap   clap   clap   clap   clap   squeeze   clap   squeeze

4. count:
clap: clap   squeeze   clap   clap   clap   squeeze   squeeze   squeeze

1. Count aloud the beats of the rhythm patterns as you point to each note.
2. Write the counts for patterns 3 and 4.
3. Clap the rhythm patterns and count aloud.
4. Play the patterns on rhythm instruments.
5. EXTRA FUN: Have a rhythm ensemble with each student playing one pattern. Repeat the pattern several times.

(MPB 24, 25)

STEPPING AND SKIPPING

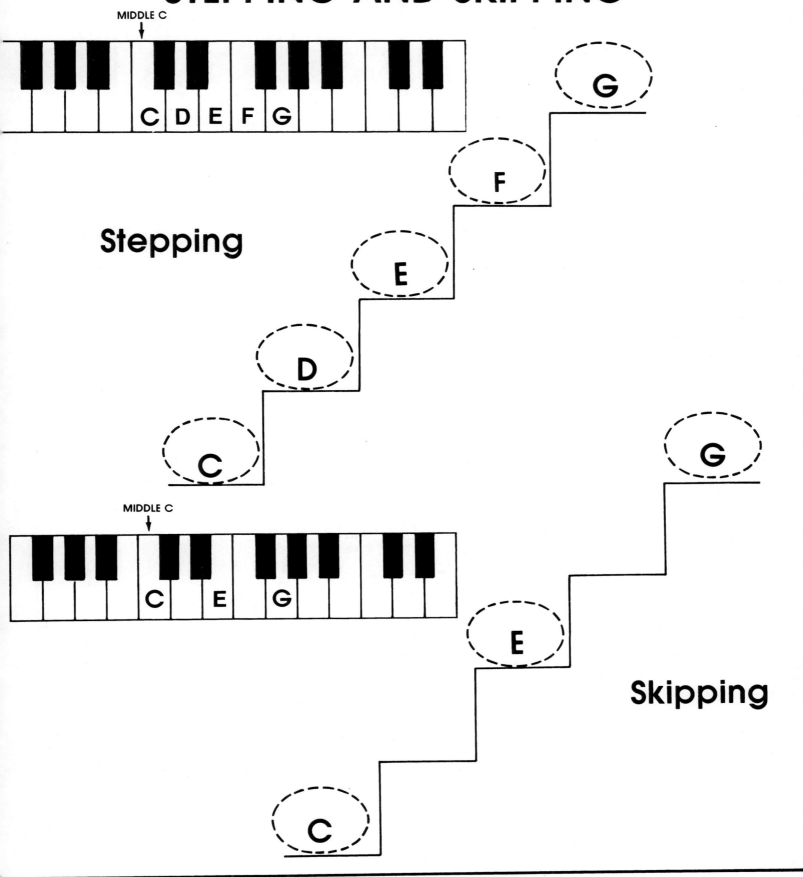

1. Draw on the dotted lines to make the stepping notes.
2. Draw on the dotted lines to make the skipping notes.
3. Practice playing skipping and stepping notes.
4. EXTRA FUN: Place right hand finger 1 on Middle C. Your teacher will say, "Step up, step up, skip down". After several calls your teacher will ask which key you are playing. Each student playing the correct note gets a marker. The student with the most markers at the end of the game is the winner.

CHARLIE'S LEFT HAND MIDDLE C

1. Draw on the dotted lines to make Charlie's Middle C note.
2. Draw a line from Charlie's Middle C note to the Middle C key on the keyboard.
3. Draw on the dotted lines to make the letter C.
4. Circle finger 1 on the left hand pictured above.
5. When Charlie's Middle C is drawn on the first line above the <u>bass clef staff</u>, you will play the key with finger 1 of your LEFT HAND. Locate Charlie's Middle C on the keyboard and play it with left hand finger 1.

(MPB 26.27)

BENJAMIN'S B

MIDDLE C

B

1. Draw on the dotted lines to make Benjamin's B note.
2. Draw a line from Benjamin's B note to the B key on the keyboard.
3. Draw on the dotted lines to make the letter B.
4. Circle finger 2 on the left hand pictured above.
5. Locate Benjamin's B on the keyboard and play it with left hand finger 2.

(MPB 28,29)

ANIKO'S A

1. Draw on the dotted lines to make Aniko's A note.
2. Draw a line from Aniko's A note to the A key on the keyboard.
3. Draw on the dotted lines to make the letter A.
4. Circle finger 3 on the left hand pictured above.
5. Locate Aniko's A on the keyboard and play it with left hand finger 3.

(MPB 30,31)

GOMEZ' LEFT HAND G

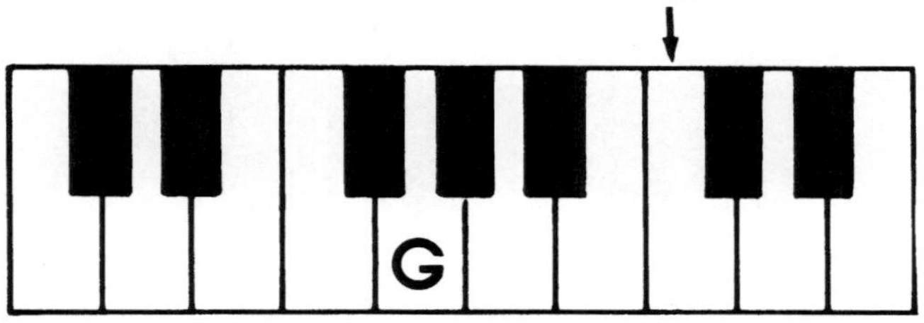

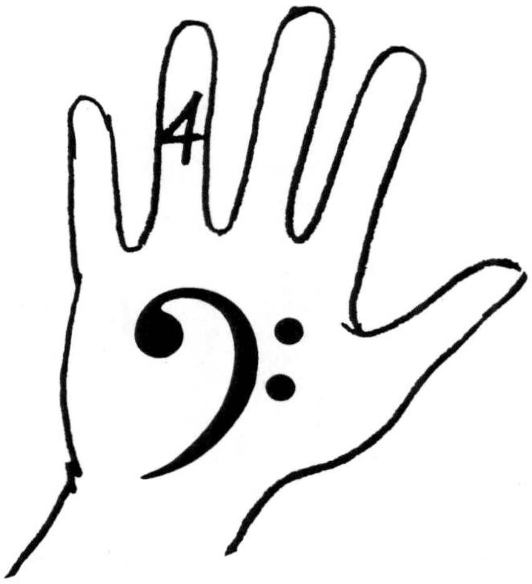

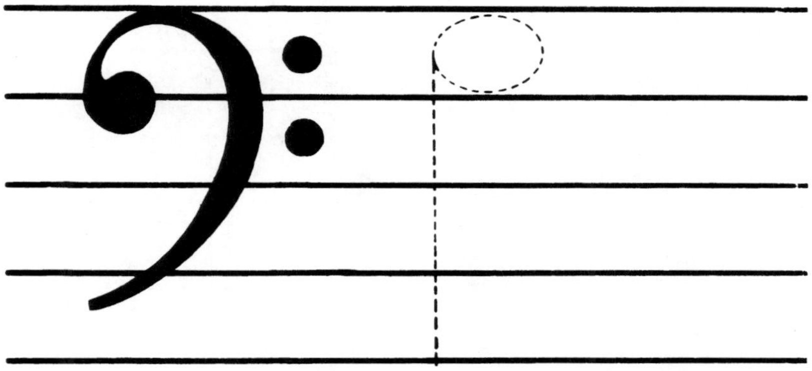

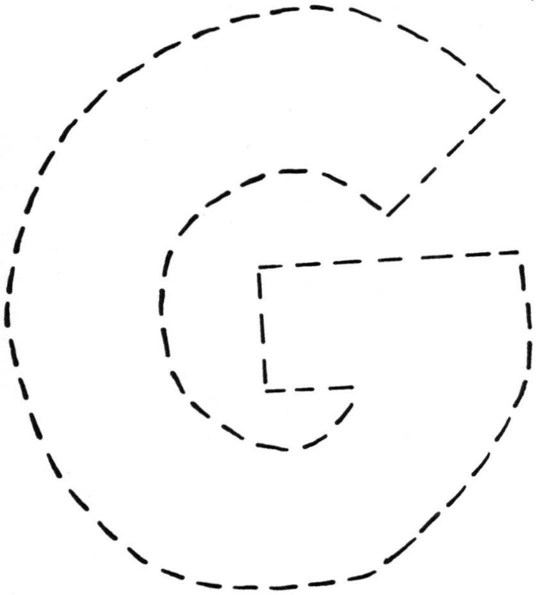

MIDDLE C

1. Draw on the dotted lines to make Gomez' G note.
2. Draw a line from Gomez' G note to the G key on the keyboard.
3. Draw on the dotted lines to make the letter G.
4. Circle finger 4 on the left hand pictured above.
5. Locate Gomez' G on the keyboard and play it with left hand finger 4.

(MPB 32-33)

Fifi's Left Hand F

1. Draw on the dotted lines to make Fifi's F note.
2. Draw a line from Fifi's F note to the F key on the keyboard.
3. Draw on the dotted lines to make the letter F.
4. Circle finger 5 on the left hand pictured above.
5. Locate Fifi's F on the keyboard and play it with left hand finger 5.

(MPB 34-35)

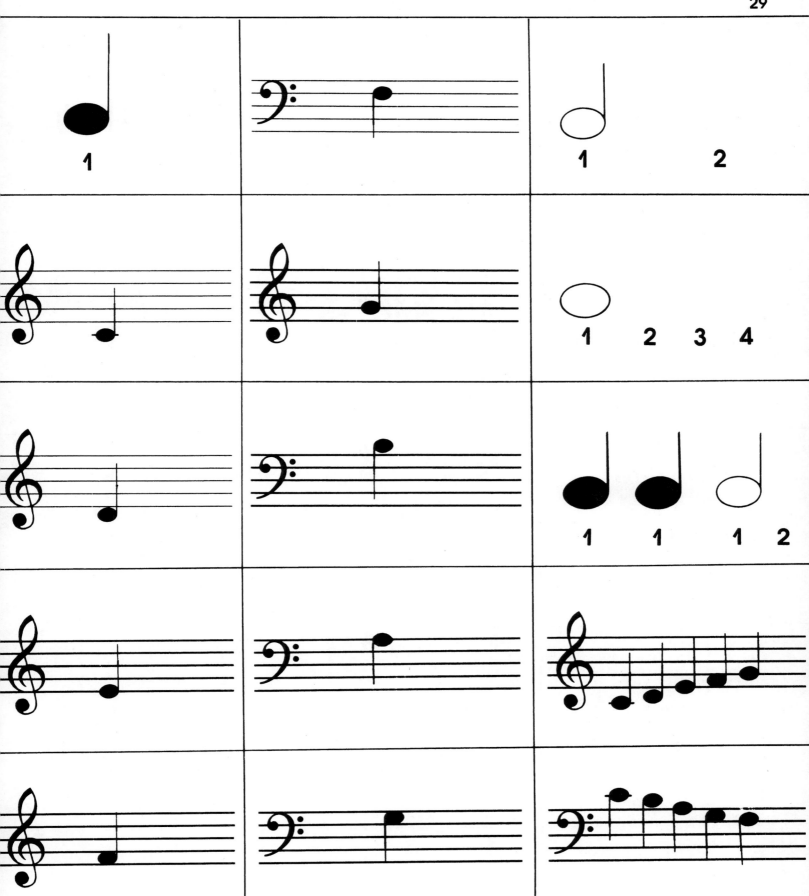

Cut out the blocks and use them as flash cards to review the things you have learned in this book.

(MPB 37)

HALF NOTE Count 1 2	**FIFI'S F** **BASS CLEF**	**QUARTER NOTE** Count 1
WHOLE NOTE Count 1 2 3 4	**GOMEZ' G** **TREBLE CLEF**	**CHARLIE'S** **MIDDLE C** **TREBLE CLEF**
QUARTER, **QUARTER** **HALF NOTE** Count 1 1 1 2	**BENJAMIN'S B** **BASS CLEF**	**DANKA'S D** **TREBLE CLEF**
Notes going up **C, D, E, F, G**	**ANIKO'S A** **BASS CLEF**	**ELLEN'S E** **TREBLE CLEF**
Notes going **down** **C, B, A, G, F**	**GOMEZ' G** **BASS CLEF**	**FIFI'S F** **TREBLE CLEF**

NOTE AND KEY REVIEW

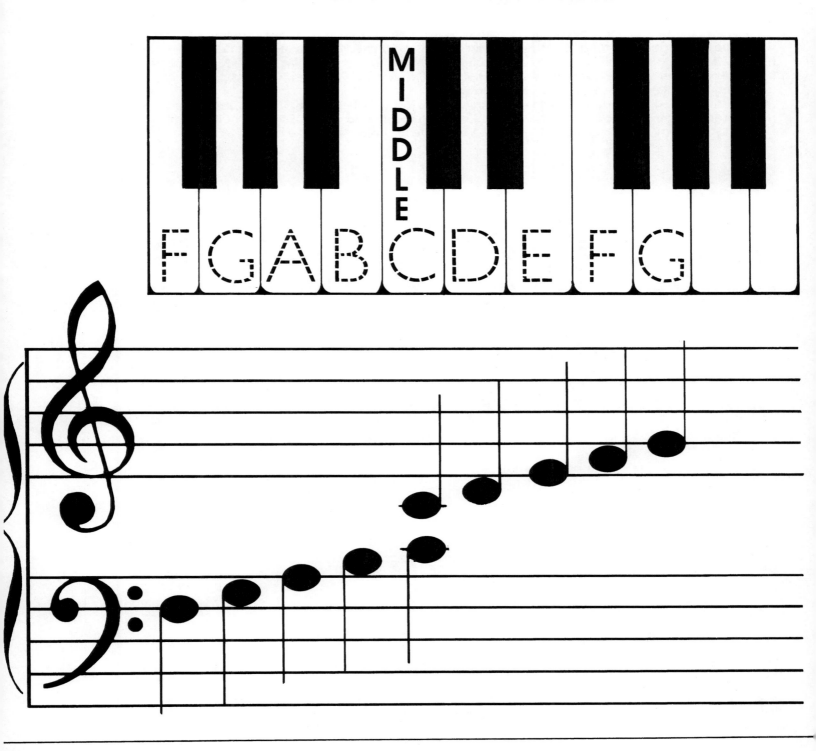

1. Draw lines from each note to the correct key.
2. Place both hands on your keyboard with both thumbs on Middle C. When your teacher calls a letter name, play the correct key.
3. EXTRA FUN: Your teacher will tell you which key to play, then will say, "Skip up, step down." After several calls your teacher will ask which key you are playing. Each student with the correct answer will get a marker. The student with the most markers at the end of the game is the winner.

(MPB 36)

Songs for Singing

TEACHER: RHYTHM INSTRUMENT or RHYTHM ENSEMBLE followed by a rhythm pattern is notated at the end of some songs. These are suggested rhythms for the students to play on rhythm instruments as the teacher plays and sings the song at the keyboard. These patterns should be introduced to the students by rote. The term RHYTHM INSTRUMENT suggests that all students play the pattern in unison. The term RHYTHM ENSEMBLE suggests that two parts be played simultaneously, with some students playing the top line (with stems pointing up) and some students playing the bottom line (with stems pointing down).

The teacher may create additional rhythm patterns for use with the songs. Existing patterns may be simplified or more challenging patterns may be introduced, depending upon the ability level of the students.

SONGS FOR HOLIDAYS AND SPECIAL OCCASIONS are on pages 40, AND 41.

Friends

STEWART - GLOVER

Moderately slow

① Char - lie is my good friend,__ Dank - a,__ too. El - len is my best friend,__

Next to you. Fi - fi is my bud - dy,__ Go - mez,__ too.

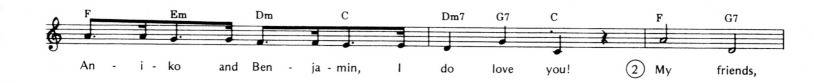

An - i - ko and Ben - ja - min, I do love you! ② My friends,

My friends, Bud - dies from be - gin - ning to the end!

POSITION: Children stand in a circle, hands joined.
DIRECTIONS: ① Circle around in time with the music, taking a step on the first and third beats.
② Join hands in pairs, swinging arms in time with the music.

RHYTHM INSTRUMENT: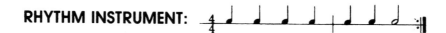

Hot Cross Buns

Traditional

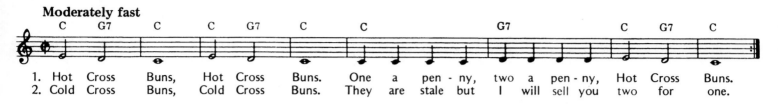

Moderately fast

1. Hot Cross Buns, Hot Cross Buns. One a pen-ny, two a pen-ny, Hot Cross Buns.
2. Cold Cross Buns, Cold Cross Buns. They are stale but I will sell you two for one.

POSITION: Each child stands alone.

DIRECTIONS: Walk around the room, holding out hands, offering to sell the hot (or cold) cross buns.

NOTE: Children may also learn to play this song on the keyboard by rote if they are ready.

I'll Just Be Me

STEWART - GLOVER

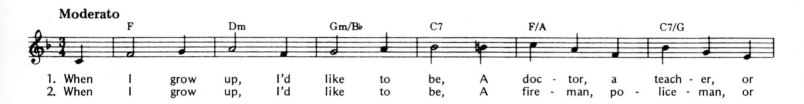

Moderato

1. When I grow up, I'd like to be, A doc - tor, a teach - er, or
2. When I grow up, I'd like to be, A fire - man, po - lice - man, or

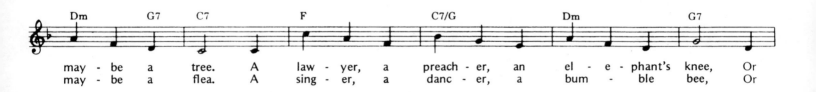

may - be a tree. A law - yer, a preach - er, an el - e - phant's knee, Or
may - be a flea. A sing - er, a danc - er, a bum - ble bee, Or

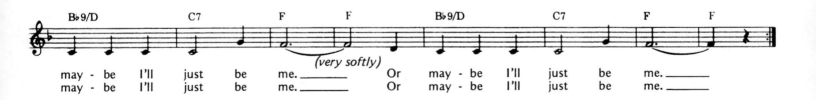

(very softly)

may - be I'll just be me._____ Or may - be I'll just be me._____
may - be I'll just be me._____ Or may - be I'll just be me._____

DIRECTIONS: Use this song to feature solo voices.

All sing: "When I grow up I'd like to be"

Solo 1: "A doctor, a teacher or maybe a tree."

Solo 2: "A lawyer, a preacher, an elephant's knee."

All: "Or maybe I'll just be me..."

RHYTHM ENSEMBLE:

Put Your Little Foot

Traditional

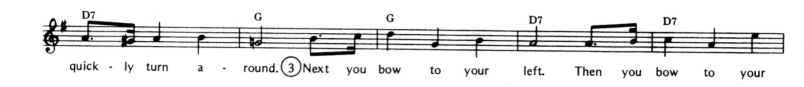

POSITION: Children stand in a circle.
DIRECTIONS: ① Tap right foot on floor. ② Join hands and circle to the right.
③ Do the actions appropriate for the words. ④ Clap hands.

Row Your Boat

Traditional

POSITION: Children sit on chairs, facing each other with hands joined.
DIRECTIONS: Rock back and forth in rhythm with the music
KEYBOARD OSTINATO: Students may play Middle C with right hand thumb throughout
the song, using a dotted quarter note rhythm.

Brother John

Traditional

Moderately fast

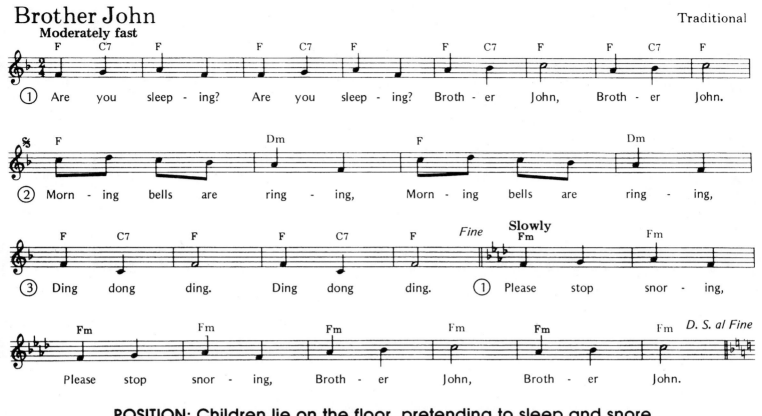

Are you sleep - ing? Are you sleep - ing? Broth - er John, Broth - er John.

Morn - ing bells are ring - ing, Morn - ing bells are ring - ing,

Ding dong ding. Ding dong ding. ① Please stop snor - ing,

Please stop snor - ing, Broth - er John, Broth - er John.

POSITION: Children lie on the floor, pretending to sleep and snore.
DIRECTIONS: ① Sing with eyes closed.
② Sit up and stretch.
③ Stand and pretend to ring bells.

RHYTHM INSTRUMENT:

London Hill

Traditional

Briskly

① As I was walk - ing up Lon - don Hill, Lon - don Hill, Lon - don Hill, As

I was walk - ing up Lon - don Hill on a cold frost - y morn - ing.

②Verse 2: I wear my gloves when the cold wind blows...
③Verse 3: I wear my coat when the cold wind blows...
④Verse 4: I wear my boots when the snow comes down...
POSITION: Each child stands alone.
DIRECTIONS: 1 Walk in rhythm with the music.
②,③,④Pretend to put on the clothes.

RHYTHM INSTRUMENT: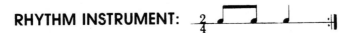

Tummy Yummies
(The Muffin Man)

Traditional

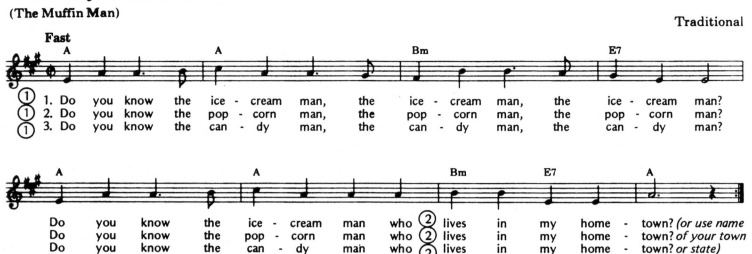

Fast

A	A	Bm	E7

① 1. Do you know the ice - cream man, the ice - cream man, the ice - cream man?
① 2. Do you know the pop - corn man, the pop - corn man, the pop - corn man?
① 3. Do you know the can - dy man, the can - dy man, the can - dy man?

A	A	Bm	E7	A

Do you know the ice - cream man who ② lives in my home - town? *(or use name*
Do you know the pop - corn man who ② lives in my home - town? *of your town*
Do you know the can - dy man who ② lives in my home - town? *or state)*

POSITION: Children stand in a circle, hands joined.
DIRECTIONS: ① Swing hands together in rhythm with the music.
② Clap hands in rhythm with the music.

RHYTHM ENSEMBLE: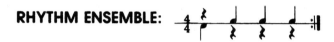

London Bridge

Traditional

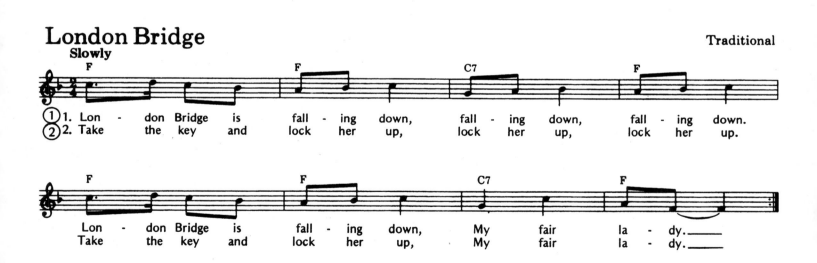

Slowly

F	F	C7	F

①1. Lon - don Bridge is fall - ing down, fall - ing down, fall - ing down.
②2. Take the key and lock her up, lock her up, lock her up.

F	F	C7	F

Lon - don Bridge is fall - ing down, My fair la - dy.____
Take the key and lock her up, My fair la - dy.____

POSITION: Two children join hands and hold them high to make a bridge.
DIRECTIONS: ① Children pass under the "bridge."
② The bridge-makers lower their hands around the child who passes
under as the bridge "falls down," and swing the child around as verse
2 is sung.

RHYTHM ENSEMBLE: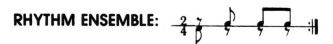

Bow, Belinda

Traditional

Slowly

1. Bow, bow, bow, Oh Be - lin - da. Bow, bow, bow, Oh Be - lin - da.

Bow, bow, bow, Oh Be - lin - da. Won't you be my part - ner?

Verse 2: Right hand up, Oh Belinda...
Verse 3: Left hand up, Oh Belinda...
Verse 4: Both hands up, Oh Belinda...
POSITION: Children face each other in pairs.
DIRECTIONS: Do the actions appropriate for the words.

RHYTHM ENSEMBLE:

Old Brass Wagon

Traditional

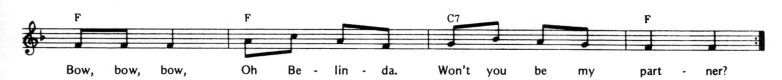
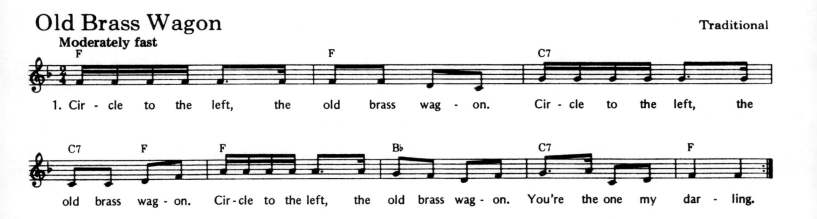

Moderately fast

1. Cir - cle to the left, the old brass wag - on. Cir - cle to the left, the

old brass wag - on. Cir - cle to the left, the old brass wag - on. You're the one my dar - ling.

Verse 2: Circle to the right, the old brass wagon...
Verse 3: Skipping 'round and 'round, the old brass wagon...
Verse 4: Clap your hands with me, the old brass wagon...
POSITION: Children stand in a circle, hands joined.
DIRECTIONS: Do the actions appropriate for the words.

RHYTHM ENSEMBLE:

Pop! Goes the Weasel

Traditional

Moderately fast

① 1. All a - round the shoe - mak - er's bench, the mon - key chased the wea - sel. The

① 2. Pen - ny for a spool of thread, a pen - ny for a nee - dle.

mon - key thought t'was all in fun. ② Pop! Goes the wea - sel.

That's the way the mon - ey goes. ② Pop! Goes the wea - sel.

POSITION: Children stand in a circle, hands joined.
DIRECTIONS: ① Skip to the right.
② Clap hands and stomp feet on the word, "Pop!"

RHYTHM ENSEMBLE:

Traveling

JAY STEWART

Fast

① 1. Red light, green light, stop and go. Cars move fast then cars move slow.

② 2. Big train mov - ing down the track. Big wheels turn - ing, clack, clack, clack.

Zoom, zoom, zoom. Beep, beep, beep. Cars go rush - ing down the street.

Choo, choo, choo. Click, click, clack. Red ca - boose is on the back.

③ 3. Fas - ten seat belts, Here we go! Air - plane fly - ing Oh so low.

Climb, climb, climb, Fly, fly, fly, High - er, high - er in the sky!

POSITION: Each child stands alone.
DIRECTIONS: ① Walk around the room, "stopping, going, moving fast, moving slowly, honking horn" as the words direct.
② Bend arms at the elbows, extending one arm forward as the other arm pushes backwards, imitating train wheels.
③ Extend arms out from the sides to form "wings". "Fly" around the room like an airplane.

RHYTHM INSTRUMENT:

My Pets

JAY STEWART

Moderately slow

1. I have a dog, his name is Frog, he sings and sings and wails. His
2. I have a cat, she is so fat, she can't get through the door. She

op - 'ra voice is the crit - ic's choice when he sings Puc - cin - i like a night-in - gale.
eats all day and at night she plays the pi - a - no like you've nev - er heard be - fore.

3. My dog Frog and my fat cat, They make a love - ly pair. My

dog Frog sings, my fat cat plays, Gee I wish I had a danc - ing po - lar bear!

POSITION: Children face each other in pairs.
DIRECTIONS: Clap hands on the first beat of each measure; clap hands against partner's hands on the third beat.

RHYTHM INSTRUMENT:

Songs for Holidays and Special Occasions

Halloween

JAY STEWART

Moderato

1. Time for ghosts and pump - kins too. Hal - low - een
2. Witch - es fly - ing on their brooms. Hal - low - een

Watch for gob - lins chas - ing you. Hal - low - een. BOO!
Black cats howl - ing at the moon. Hal - low - een. YOWL!

POSITION: Children stand alone.
DIRECTIONS: Children "creep" around the room, scaring one another on the words, "Boo" and "Yowl".

RHYTHM INSTRUMENT:

Prayer for Thanksgiving

STEWART - GLOVER

Slowly

Thank you for food and for lov - ing care. Thank you for friends that we all can share.

Thank you for mu - sic and songs to sing. Thank you, oh, thank you for ev - 'ry - thing.

KEYBOARD OSTINATO: C above Middle C may be played or sung in quarter note rhythm throughout this song as an ostinato accompaniment. When singing the ostinato, the words, "Thank You", may be repeated throughout the song.

RHYTHM ENSEMBLE:

Christmas Fantasy

JAY STEWART

Brightly

Christ - mas Day is com - ing soon! Time to fill the stock - ings.

*Cakes and cook - ies, can - dies too, Lots of love from me to you.
*Balls and bats and doll - ies, too,

* Encourage the children to create words of their own for this phrase.

RHYTHM ENSEMBLE:

Valentine

DAVID CARR GLOVER

Moderato

Val - en - tine, Val - en - tine, Will you be my Val - en - tine?

I'll be yours, You be mine. Come and be my Val - en - tine.

RHYTHM ENSEMBLE:

St. Patrick's Day

STEWART - GLOVER

Moderately fast

There's a ① lit - tle green man who lives in the green woods and he

wears a green hat and two fun - ny green shoes. Now as ② ev - 'ry - one knows, you must

wear your green clothes or the lit - tle green man pinch - y win - cy your nose! It's Saint Pat - rick's Day, Yeah!

KEYBOARD OSTINATO: Students may play the descending C Major Scale beginning on C above Middle C. Right hand finger 2 may be played on each key in half note (♩) rhythm. Begin playing the scale at Number ① . Repeat the scale beginning at ② .

Easter Bunny

STEWART - GLOVER

Moderato

East - er bas - ket, East - er bas - ket, emp - ty as can be. Will that spe - cial

East - er bun - ny leave some treats for me? I would like some jel - ly beans, a

ba - by chick - y too. Lots of col - ored East - er eggs, a bun - ny just like you.

RHYTHM ENSEMBLE:

Program Guide of Concepts and Activities for

	CONCEPTS			ACTIVITIES - MY PIANO BOOK A		
Program	Note Reading	Rhythm Reading	Keyboard Recognition	Performance	Finger Exercises (See (1) Below)	Ear Training
I	Middle C, D	♩ ♩ ♩|♩ ♩ ♩|♩|| Teacher: Rhythm patterns should be drawn on poster board or chalkboard. Teacher points to notes as students count aloud and (1) clap the patterns, (2) play on rhythm instruments, or (3) play at keyboard on a single key or on a 2 or 3-note chord.	All C's, and D's.	Pp. 4, 5 - review. Introduce pp. 6, 7, 8, 9. Teacher: Discuss pictures of Charlie and Danka; get students involved with each character.	♩ ♩ ♩|♩ ♩ ♩|♩ ♩ ♪ RH 1 1 1 1 1 1 1 LH 5 5 5 5 5 5 5 RH 2 2 2 2 2 2 2 LH 4 4 4 4 4 4 4 RH 1 1 1 1 2 2 2 LH 5 5 5 5 4 4 4 Teacher: See (1) below for finger exercise directions.	Sing and play p. 39, No. 1 in imitation of the teacher. Teacher: Ear training directions are on p. 38 of MY PIANO BOOK A.
II	Middle C, D	♩ ♩|♩ ♩ ♩|♩|| ♩ ♩|♩ ♩ ♩||	All C's, and D's.	Review p. 9; Introduce pp. 10, 11.	RH 1 1 2 2 3 3 3 LH 5 5 4 4 3 3 3 RH 3 3 2 2 1 1 1 LH 3 3 4 4 5 5 5 RH 1 1 2 2 3 2 1 LH 5 5 4 4 3 4 5	Sing and play p. 39, No. 2 in imitation, No. 1 by ear.
III	Middle C, D, E	♩ ♩ ♩ ♩| ♩ ♩ || ♩ ♩ ♩ ♩|♩ ♩||	All C's, D's and E's.	Review p. 11; Introduce pp. 12, 13, 14, 15.	RH 1 2 3 2 1 1 1 LH 5 4 3 4 5 5 5 RH 3 2 1 2 3 3 3 LH 3 4 5 4 3 3 3 RH 1 3 1 3 1 1 1 LH 5 3 5 3 5 5 5	Sing and play p. 39, No. 3 in imitation, No. 2 by ear.

Teacher: This material is divided into seven programs, each dealing with specific integrated concepts. <u>Do not consider one program to be one lesson.</u> Adjust the programs to meet the specific needs of your class. The time needed to cover the material will depend upon several factors, including the maturity of the students, whether the lesson is private or group, and whether the parents attend the lesson.

(1) FINGER EXERCISES - All exercises should be played with the right hand (RH) finger 1 on Middle C and the left hand (LH) finger 5 on C below Middle C unless otherwise stated. The teacher should play and sing finger numbers at the keyboard, then the students should play and sing the finger numbers at the keyboard in imitation of the teacher (see the procedure for imitation playing, MY PIANO BOOK A, p. 38). The process should be repeated, with teacher and students playing and singing key names. The patterns should be kept rhythmically simple (basic quarter note pulse) as shown in the first finger exercise above. Students may play hands separate or hands together if ready. Additional patterns may be created by the teacher.

MY PIANO BOOK A and MY COLOR AND PLAY BOOK A

ACTIVITIES - MY COLOR AND PLAY BOOK A			
Concept Awareness	Songs to Sing	Listening Suggestions	Suggested Parent Activities
Pp. 3, 4, 5, 6, 7, 8, 9.	FRIENDS, p. 32 I'LL JUST BE ME, p. 33 Teacher: Songs for holidays and special occasions are on pp. 40, 41	1.AFRICAN DANCE SONG, Congo 2.TEDDY BEAR MARCH, Bratten 3.THE WOODS AT NIGHT, Brahms Teacher: All selections are recorded on THE SMALL DANCER (#391), THE SMALL PLAYER (#392) and THE SMALL LISTENER (#393). See (2) below.	The activity suggestions given here apply to all the programs. The teacher will suggest specific activities for lesson or concept reinforcement. Share practice time with your child everyday. Make it a happy time of sharing the things your child is learning. Encourage and praise your child. Singing is one of the best ways to develop a good musical ear. Encourage the child to sing. Sing with the child - you'll both enjoy it. Help the child learn the words to the singing songs and the keyboard songs.
Pp. 10, 11, 13.	HOT CROSS BUNS, p. 33. PUT YOUR LITTLE FOOT, p. 34.	1.CIRCUS MARCH, Fucik-Laurendeau 2.WALTZ, Strauss 3.LITTLE MUSIC BOX, Maykapar	Listen to music with your child. Listen to the radio, records, live performances - take advantage of every opportunity to share listening time. Talk about the things you hear, about the feelings the music creates. (Does it make you sad, happy, excited?)
Pp. 12, 14, 15, 16.	ROW YOUR BOAT, p. 34. BROTHER JOHN, p. 35.	1.OUT OF THE FOG, Raymond 2.CHILDREN'S POLKA 3.ON HORSEBACK, Gretchaninoff	Help your child make simple rhythm instruments to use at home. Drum: cut the ends from a coffee can and put the plastic cover over one end. Triangle: suspend a large nail from a string; strike with another nail. Sticks: use wooden dowels.

TEACHER: An example of a WEEKLY LESSON PLAN based upon this program guide is on page 46.

(2) THE SMALL MUSICIAN SERIES, compiled, written, and edited by Roberta McLaughlin and Lucille Wood, is highly recommended. The series consists of a delightful song book, THE SMALL SINGER, with two records of the songs, and three additional recordings titled THE SMALL LISTENER, THE SMALL PLAYER, and THE SMALL DANCER. The song book and all recordings include suggested activities for the teacher. The series is listed in the Bowmar catalogue and may be ordered from:

Belwin-Mills Publishing Corp.

Program Guide of Concepts and Activities for

	CONCEPTS			ACTIVITIES - MY PIANO BOOK A		
Program	Note Reading	Rhythm Reading	Keyboard Recognition	Performance	Finger Exercises (See (1) Below)	Ear Training
IV	Middle C, D, E, F	♩ ♩♩ ♩♩ ♩‖ ♩♩♩♩ ♩♩♩‖	All C's, D's, E's, and F's.	Review p. 15. Introduce pp. 16, 17, 18, 19.	RH 1 1 2 2 3 3 4 LH 5 5 4 4 3 3 2 RH 4 4 3 3 2 2 1 LH 2 2 3 3 4 4 5 RH 1 2 3 4 3 2 1 LH 5 4 3 2 3 4 5	Sing and play p. 39, No. 4 in imitation, No. 3 by ear.
V	Middle C, D, E, F, G	♩♩♩♩ ○ ‖ ♩ ♩ ○ ‖	All C's, D's, E's, F's, and G's.	Review p. 19. Introduce pp. 20, 21, 22, 23, 24, 25.	RH 1 2 3 4 5 5 5 LH 5 4 3 2 1 1 1 RH 5 4 3 2 1 1 1 LH 1 2 3 4 5 5 5 RH 1 2 3 4 5 3 1 LH 5 4 3 2 1 3 5	Sing and play p. 39, No. 5 in imitation, No. 4 by ear.
VI	Middle C, D, E, F, G B, A, G below Middle C	○ ♩ ♩ ♩ ♩‖ ♩♩♩ ♩ ○ ‖	All keys, A, B, C, D, E, F, G	Review pp. 24, 25. Introduce pp. 26, 27, 28, 29, 30, 31, 32, 33.	Both thumbs on Middle C, hands separate. RH 1 1 2 2 3 4 5 LH 1 2 3 4 5 5 5 RH 5 5 4 4 3 2 1 LH 5 4 3 2 1 1 1 RH 1 1 3 3 5 5 5 LH 1 2 3 4 5 3 1	Sing and play p. 39, No. 5 in imitation and by ear. Review Nos. 1, 2, 3, 4 in imitation and by ear.
VII	Middle C, D, E, F, G, B, A, G, F, below Middle C	○ ♩ ♩ ♩ ‖ ○ ♩ ♩♩‖	Review all keys, A, B, C, D, E, F, G	Review pp. 32, 33. Introduce pp. 34, 35, 36, 37.	Both thumbs on Middle C, hands separate. RH 1 3 5 4 3 2 1 LH 5 5 4 4 3 2 1 RH 5 3 1 3 5 3 1 LH 1 1 2 2 3 4 5 RH 1 5 4 3 2 1 1 LH 1 5 4 3 2 1 1	Review p. 39, Nos. 1, 2, 3, 4, 5 in imitation and by ear.

MY PIANO BOOK A and MY COLOR AND PLAY BOOK A

ACTIVITIES - MY COLOR AND PLAY BOOK A			
Concept Awareness	Songs to Sing	Listening Suggestions	Suggested Parent Activities
P. 17. Review p. 7.	LONDON HILL, p. 35. TUMMY YUMMIES, p. 36.	1.JUMPING JACK, Niehaus 2.MARY HAD A LITTLE LAMB 3. DANCE OF THE WARRIORS, Hanson	Clapping, moving to music, playing rhythm instruments, doing actions to songs - all of these activities help develop the child's motor skills. Help the child learn the actions to the songs being used at the lesson. Songs with the words, music and actions are in MY COLOR AND PLAY BOOK A pages 32-35.
Pp. 18, 19, 20 , 21, 22, 23.	LONDON BRIDGE, p. 36. BOW, BELINDA, p. 37.	1.INDIAN DANCE SONG, Sioux 2.POP! GOES THE WEASEL 3.MARCH, Haydn 4.POLKA, Strauss	Let the child practice drawing the notes and symbols learned at the lesson. Flash cards are easy to make. Cut cards from cardboard or colored paper. Use the symbols pictured in the books as patterns and draw the symbols on the cards. Let the child help with making the cards. Make up games to play with the cards to reinforce what is being taught at the lesson.
Pp. 24, 25, 26, 27.	OLD BRASS WAGON, p. 37. POP! GOES THE WEASEL, p. 38.	1.GRASSHOPPERS, Raymond 2. SI SEÑOR, Latin American Dance 3. CHIAPANECAS, Mexico 4. THE SMUGGLERS, Taylor	Allow your child's natural creativity to express itself. Encourage your child to explore the many sounds that can be made on the piano (or other instruments). Imitate various sounds at the keyboard: music box, animal sounds, raindrops, thunder. Review the songs in MY PIANO BOOK A. Have the student perform the songs for the family in a mini-recital.
Pp. 28, 29, 30, 31.	TRAVELING, p. 38. MY PETS, p. 39.	1.HUKILAU, Hawaii 2.COUNTRY DANCE, American Folk 3.MARCH, Beethoven 4.FRIGHTENING,Schumann	

The CASSETTE TAPE RECORDING of the MUSIC READINESS SERIES includes all the keyboard and singing songs.

LESSON PLAN GUIDE
ELEMENTS OF A LESSON PLAN

SINGING
Songs they know and enjoy singing.
New songs.
Songs for holidays and special occasions.
Applying rhythm ensembles and movements to songs.

REINFORCEMENT ACTIVITIES
Using activities which require skills already studied.
Repetition.

CHECKING HOMEWORK ASSIGNMENT
Checking written work.
Hearing keyboard assignments.

KEYBOARD
Songs to play.
Rhythm patterns to play.
Ensemble playing.
Imitation playing.
Finger exercises.

NOTE READING
Singing note names of keyboard songs using flash cards for note recognition.

EAR TRAINING
Singing in imitation and by ear.
Playing in imitation and by ear.

RHYTHM READING
Rhythm charts.
Drawing rhythm patterns on chalkboard.

LISTENING ACTIVITIES
Hearing the teacher play and sing.
Hearing recordings (create a listening corner.)
Carpet samples make excellent "sit-up-ons"

HOME ASSIGNMENT
Activities to be done before the next lesson time.

GOODBYE
It is good to have something special to signal the end of the lesson. When the students hear the signal (a song is easy to use) they put away whatever they are doing and get ready to sing the GOODBYE SONG.

SAMPLE LESSON PLAN FOR
MY COLOR AND PLAY BOOK A AND MY PIANO BOOK A

DID YOU EVER SEE A LASSIE? (MFMB-45)
ROW YOUR BOAT (MCPB-A-34)
Teach words by imitation. Add movements.

Today the class starts a new book.
Read the introduction on page 4, of MPB-A.
Name and explain all the symbols on pages 4 and 5 of MPB-A.
Complete **MY MUSIC REVIEW** (MCPB-A-3-5)

Introduce Charlie (MPB-A-6). What is Charlie doing? Complete the activities in MCPB-A-6. Develop the character; get students interested and involved with Charlie.

Teach **CHARLIE'S SONG** (MPB-A-7)
Have students:
   a) Clap hands and sing words.
   b) Play rhythm instruments and sing words.
   c) Clap and count aloud as teacher points to notes.
   d) Play and sing words.

Have students sing ear training pattern.
Use Line I (MPB-A-39). Students may play pattern if they are ready.

Point to notes on rhythm chart as students clap or play rhythm instruments and count aloud.

THE WOODS AT NIGHT by Brahms.
Use suggested activities on record.

1) MPB-A-7 Sing, clap and play **CHARLIE'S SONG.**
2) Sing **FRIENDS** and **I'LL JUST BE ME** (MCPB-A-32-33)
3) Use directions in MPB-A-6 to locate and play all the C's on your keyboard.

Teach **HOT CROSS BUNS** (MCPB-A-33) by imitation.
Sing **GOODBYE SONG** (MFMB-31)

NOTE: The order of activities in the lesson plan should be arranged to best achieve the lesson goals. It is important to vary the activities; the young child has a short attention span. Change often from quiet activities to activities including body movement, i.e., coloring, singing with motions, listening, playing rhythm instruments.

This certificate is presented to

_____

In Recognition of the
Successful Completion of

**My Color and
Play Book A**

By Betty Glasscock
and Jay Stewart
in collaboration with
DAVID CARR GLOVER

Teacher _____

Date _____